The Sayings

The Sayings Series

Jane Austen
Charlotte Brontë
Lord Byron
Lewis Carroll
Winston Churchill
Charles Dickens
Benjamin Disraeli
F. Scott Fitzgerald
Benjamin Franklin
Goethe
Thomas Hardy
Henrik Ibsen
Dr Johnson
James Joyce
John Keats
Rudyard Kipling
D.H. Lawrence
Somerset Maugham
Friedrich Nietzsche
George Orwell
Dorothy Parker
Samuel Pepys
Ezra Pound
Sir Walter Scott
William Shakespeare
George Bernard Shaw
Sydney Smith
R.L. Stevenson
Jonathan Swift
Leo Tolstoy
Anthony Trollope
Mark Twain
Evelyn Waugh
Oscar Wilde
Virginia Woolf
W.B. Yeats
The Bible
The Buddha
Jesus
Moses
Muhammad

The Sayings of

LEWIS
CARROLL

edited by
Robert Pearce

DUCKWORTH

First published in 1996 by
Gerald Duckworth & Co. Ltd.
The Old Piano Factory
48 Hoxton Square, London N1 6PB
Tel: 0171 729 5986
Fax: 0171 729 0015

A catalogue record for this book
is available from the British Library

ISBN 0 7156 2743 0

Typeset by Ray Davies
Printed in Great Britain by
Redwood Books Ltd, Trowbridge

Contents

7 Introduction

13 Etiquette

16 Legal Proceedings

18 Words

23 Children & Adults

26 Poetry, Books & Writing

29 Boasts, Exclamations & Exhortations

33 Ironies

38 Logic & Philosophy

45 Eating & Drinking

47 Dancing & General Jubilation

48 Religion & Morality

52 On Himself

54 Animals & Plants

59 Love & Pleasure

61 Nonsense & Riddles

Introduction

Justly has it been said that 4 July 1862 is as memorable a date for English literature as 4 July 1776 for the history of the United States of America. On this 'golden afternoon' the Reverend Charles Lutwidge Dodgson (1832-98), together with another Oxford don, invited the three young daughters of the Dean of Christ Church for a picnic upstream from Folly Bridge on the Isis. To amuse his young guests Dodgson began to tell the story of 'Alice's Adventures Under Ground'. After a request from the youngest daughter, Alice, aged ten, that he should commit the story to paper, he stayed up almost the whole night and produced what, via 'Alice's Hour in Elfland', soon became the immortal *Alice's Adventures in Wonderland*. By the same process Charles Dodgson was transformed, by way of 'Edgar U.C. Westhall', into Lewis Carroll.

Enhanced by the illustrations of Sir John Tenniel, and soon coupled with a sequel (*Through the Looking-Glass and What Alice Found There*), the *Adventures* is one of the most popular children's books ever written – and the one most widely quoted by adults. It is also one of the world's most translated books: there are Gaelic, Esperanto, Braille, Swahili and many, many more versions, including two shorthand editions, six Chinese and four Japanese.

At first sight, the success and universal appeal of the Alice books is hard to fathom. Written for the Liddell girls, they were highly personal and obscurely allusive. Dodgson himself (or the stammering 'Do-Do-Dodgson') was the Dodo (and the White Knight in *Through the Looking-Glass*). The three sisters were there as well, Alice of course having her own name, as was the Oxford don, Duckworth, as the Duck. The songs and poems were burlesques upon contemporary works, now mostly forgotten. That most parodied poem in the English language, 'The Walrus and the Carpenter', was itself a parody. The Bat was the distinguished professor of mathematics Bartholomew Price, whose lectures were wondered at, with suitable perplexity, by his students. The Mad Hatter was Theophilus Carter, an Oxford furniture dealer who always wore a top hat and whose inventions included an 'alarm clock bed', unveiled at the Great Exhibition of 1851, which duly threw the sleeper onto the floor at the appointed time.

In fact, the Alice books have spawned a whole academic industry. Biographers reveal the allusions to Carroll's own experiences. Political historians point to the references to contemporary events (so that the Lion and the Unicorn represent Gladstone and Disraeli), and art historians identify the Dormouse as Dante Gabriel Rossetti's pet wombat. Scientists draw obscure parallels, so that Wonderland illustrates both the diminishing and expanding universe theories, while the Tea Party, at which it is always six o'clock, becomes De Sitter's model of the eternally still cosmos. Mathematicians insist that the 'grin without a cat' is a paradigm of pure mathematics. Psychoanalysts use the book as a sexual playground of libidinal phenomena, and philosophers employ it to explore the limits of rationality. (Most non-philosophers, however, experience again and again the delicious uncertainty of whether Carroll was being perfectly logical or idiotically ironic and humorous!)

Yet it is a poor sort of book that cannot predict the future. Perhaps the Hatter was not an awakened Theophilus but a middle-aged, twentieth-century Bertrand Russell, alongside J.M.E. McTaggart and G.E. Moore as the Dormouse and March Hare respectively. Tenniel's drawings seem to confirm at any rate Bertie's identity, though the case for the other members of Cambridge's Mad Tea Party is still open to some philosophical doubt.

Yet, academics apart, most people love the Alice

books for their delightful and ingenious combinations of fantasy and realism, for their exuberant humour and whimsey, for their word-play and their parody, for making logic into a laugh, philosophy into fun and *Weltanschauung* into a whiz. The books are unique because their author was unique. Lewis Carroll was a mathematician and logician, the sort of man who prescribed mental arithmetic as a cure for impure thoughts, as well as a devotee of puzzles, acrostics and 'language games'. (He made two anagrams of 'William Ewart Gladstone': 'Wilt tear down *all* images?' and 'Wild agitator! Means well.') He was also a poet, humorist and odd-ball (who but he would extend the pathetic fallacy to angles and parallelograms?); a linguistic philosopher who delighted in nonsense; and a lover of all children (except boys).

In short, he was one of the great Victorian eccentrics. For instance, he devised a way of ensuring that the pairing of opponents in tournaments was really fair, so that the best two players would not meet each other before the final. Einstein could no doubt have managed its complexities satisfactorily, and the more able chartered accountants would have had a sporting chance. But for ordinary mortals it was a non-starter. Similarly, he devised a cataloguing system, complete with elaborate cross-references, for all the letters he sent or received, involving a précis of almost 100,000 items. The result was that he fell years behind with his correspondence, though the voluminous catalogue was precisely accurate. He also invented a 'nyctograph', his device for making (illegible) notes in the night; and he kept detailed diagrams of where people sat and what they ate when they dined with him, so that the same people should not sit together twice or be served the same dish.

As might be expected of so singular a character, Dodgson had been blessed with a good share of disadvantages. A fairly solitary child who stammered badly, he had been bullied at Rugby by more standard boys. ('If I could have been secure from annoyance at night,' he recalled, 'the hardships of the daily life would have been comparative trifles to bear.') Moreover he committed the public school sin of being poor at games. He played cricket only once, and on bowling a single ball (which, apparently, would have been a wide had it travelled far enough) was summarily taken off. But he knew that the uses of adversity were sweet. Certainly he achieved academic success, including an Oxford First in Mathematics; and in 1852 he became a Student (i.e. Fellow) of Christ Church, a position which would be his for life so long as he remained unmarried and took holy orders.

By all accounts he was, like all the best academics, a tediously dull lecturer. He had little taste for 'goading unwilling men to learning they have no taste for'. Most colleagues also found him dull and uninteresting, overly pedantic, even by Oxford's exalted standards, and reserved to a fault. Yet there never seemed any likelihood that he would be forced to leave Christ Church. In 1861 he duly became a deacon, and marriage was never a real possibility. There was speculation, at one stage, that he had taken a fancy to Miss Prickett, governess to the children of the Dean of Christ Church, Dr Liddell; and on another occasion his name was linked with that of the teenage actress Ellen Terry. But such rumours were without foundation. As Ellen Terry wrote in her autobiography, 'He was as fond of me as he could be of anyone over the age of ten'; and in fact it was not Miss Prickett who attracted his interest but the Liddell girls themselves, and especially Alice.

Children, the Reverend Dodgson once wrote, were 'three-quarters of my life'. He had a series of 'child-friends', whom he would entertain and correspond with. Indeed he wrote them many thousands of inimitable letters. He liked kissing young girls; he took some on holiday, usually to Eastbourne; he photographed them in night-gowns; and in 1878-80 he did a number of nude studies, before parental complaints led him to abandon the practice. Not that there was any greater impropriety than this, and certainly no hint of scandal. In later life dozens of his young friends recalled how greatly they had appreciated his kindness and attention.

Only with girls did he really come alive, and only with them did he prove himself a good teacher. He was able to enter emotionally into their world, and to communicate with them in a fashion which most adults cannot begin to emulate. Hence it is Lewis Carroll's children's books which have stood the test of time, not the mathematical works of Charles Dodgson. Even so, Carroll was never able to repeat the success of the Alice books. The two *Sylvie and Bruno* volumes (1889 and 1893) now seem tedious, with their babyish burble, as well as overly moralistic, so that only the intrepid Saying-hunter is likely to wade through their entire length.

Lewis Carroll has left enduring masterpieces in *Alice in Wonderland* and *Through the Looking-Glass* and in some of his nonsense poetry. The very private, somewhat austere and unapproachable Oxford don, who was always soberly concerned with Logic, Reason and Morality (not to mention Ambition, Distraction, Uglification, and Derision), was able to give full rein to his glorious sense of humour and perception of the absurd. We can but chortle at his galumphing, as at the Snark, the frumious Bandersnatch and even – with extreme care and attention – the Boojum. Certain it is that without him the Oxford English Dictionary would be depleted and we would be the poorer.

R.D.P.

Sources

Alice's Adventures in Wonderland
Through the Looking-Glass, and What Alice Saw There
The Hunting of the Snark
Sylvie and Bruno
Sylvie and Bruno Concluded
Symbolic Logic
The Game of Logic
Pillow Problems
A Tangled Tale
Stuart Dodgson Collingwood, *The Life and Letters of Lewis Carroll* (1898)

Etiquette

If everybody minded their own business … the world
would go round a deal faster than it does.

Alice in Wonderland

Don't grunt … that's not at all a proper way of
expressing yourself.   *Ibid.*

'I don't like the look of it at all,' said the King: 'however,
it may kiss my hand, if it likes.'   *Ibid.*

A cat may look at a king.   *Ibid.*

You look a little shy: let me introduce you to that leg of
mutton … 'Alice – Mutton: Mutton – Alice.'

Through the Looking-Glass

'May I give you a slice?' she said, taking up the knife
and fork, and looking from one Queen to the other.
'Certainly not,' the Red Queen said very decidedly: 'it
isn't etiquette to cut anyone you've been introduced to.
Remove the joint!'   *Ibid.*

'What impertinence!' said the Pudding. 'I wonder
how you'd like it, if I were to cut a slice out of you, you
creature!'
It spoke in a thick, suety sort of voice.

Ibid.

Make a remark … It's ridiculous to leave all the
conversation to the pudding!

Ibid.

Curtsey while you're thinking what to say. It saves time.

Ibid.

Look up, speak nicely, and don't twiddle your fingers all the time.   *Ibid.*

If you think we're wax-works ... you ought to pay, you know. Wax-works weren't made to be looked at for nothing.   *Ibid.*

Always speak the truth – think before you speak – and write it down afterwards.

Ibid.

To use a fork with your soup, intimating at the same time to your hostess that you are reserving the spoon for the beefsteaks, is a practice wholly exploded.

Hints for Etiquette

In proceeding to the dining-room, the gentleman gives one arm to the lady he escorts – it is unusual to offer both.   *Ibid.*

On meat being placed before you, there is no possible objection to your eating it, if so disposed; still, in all such delicate cases, be guided entirely by the conduct of those around you.   *Ibid.*

It is always allowable to ask for artichoke jelly with your boiled venison; however, there are houses where this is not supplied.

Ibid.

The method of helping roast turkey with two carving-forks is practicable, but deficient in grace.

Ibid.

We do not recommend the practice of eating cheese with a knife and fork in one hand, and a spoon and wine-glass in the other; there is a kind of awkwardness in the action which no amount of practice can entirely dispel.   *Ibid.*

As a general rule, do not kick the shins of the opposite
gentleman under the table, if personally unacquainted
with him; your pleasantry is liable to be misunderstood –
a circumstance at all times unpleasant.   *Ibid.*

Mutton first, mechanics afterwards.

A Tangled Tale

Don't fill *more* than a page and a half with apologies for
not having written sooner!

Wise Words About Letter Writing

Never, never, dear Madam (n.b. this remark is addressed
to ladies *only*: no *man* would ever do such a thing), put
'Wednesday', simply, as the date!   *Ibid.*

A Postscript is a very useful invention: but it is *not* meant
(as so many ladies suppose) to contain the real *gist* of the
letter.   *Ibid.*

Never stew your sister.

Useful and Instructive Poetry

> Learn well your grammar,
> And never stammer,
> Write well and neatly,
> And sing most sweetly,
> Be enterprising,
> Love early rising,
> Go walk of six miles,
> Have ready quick smiles,
> With winsome laughter,
> Soft flowing after.   *Life and Letters*

> Shut doors behind you
> (Don't slam them, mind you.)
>
> *Ibid.*

Roar not lest thou be abolished.   *Ibid.*

Legal Proceedings

Off with his head!

Alice in Wonderland

> The Queen of Hearts, she made some tarts,
> All on a summer day:
> The Knave of Hearts, he stole those tarts,
> And took them quite away!

Ibid.

The executioner's argument was, that you couldn't cut off a head unless there was a body to cut it off from: that he had never had to do such a thing before, and that he wasn't going to begin at his time of life. The King's argument was that anything that had a head could be beheaded, and that you weren't to talk nonsense. The Queen's argument was that, if something wasn't done about it in less than no time, she'd have everybody executed, all round.

Ibid.

Either you or your head must be off, and that in about half no time.

Ibid.

'Talking of axes,' said the Duchess, 'chop off her head!'

Ibid.

Give your evidence ... and don't be nervous, or I'll have you executed on the spot.

Ibid.

Give your evidence ... or I'll have you executed, whether you are nervous or not.

Ibid.

You must remember ... or I'll have you executed.

Ibid.

Sentence first – verdict afterwards.

Ibid.

Here one of the guinea-pigs cheered, and was
immediately suppressed by the officers of the court.

Ibid.

'I'll be judge, I'll be jury,' said the cunning old Fury;
'I'll try the whole cause and condemn you to death.'

Ibid.

'In my youth,' said his father, 'I took to the law,
And argued each case with my wife;
And the muscular strength, which it gave to my jaw,
Has lasted the rest of my life.'

Ibid.

When you are really *anxious* to impress a criminal with a
sense of his guilt, you ought not to pronounce the
sentence with your lips *quite* close to his cheek – since a
kiss at the end of it, however accidental, weakens the
effect terribly.

Sylvie and Bruno

When all are guilty, none should play the Judge.

Prologues to Plays

Words

'*Un*important, of course, I meant,' the King hastily said, and went on to himself in an undertone, 'important – unimportant – unimportant – important – ' as if he were trying which word sounded best.   *Alice in Wonderland*

Take care of the senses and the sounds will take care of themselves.   *Ibid.*

Did you ever see such a thing as a drawing of a muchness?   *Ibid.*

'And how many hours a day did you do lessons?' said Alice ...

'Ten hours the first day,' said the Mock Turtle: 'nine the next, and so on.'

'What a curious plan!' exclaimed Alice.

'That's the reason they're called lessons,' the Gryphon remarked: 'because they lessen from day to day.'

Ibid.

'I only took the regular course.'

'What was that?' inquired Alice.

'Reeling and Writhing, of course, to begin with,' the Mock Turtle replied; 'and then the different branches of Arithmetic – Ambition, Distraction, Uglification, and Derision.'   *Ibid.*

'When I use a word', Humpty Dumpty said, in rather a scornful tone, 'it means just what I choose it to mean – neither more nor less.'

'The question is', said Alice, 'whether you *can* make words mean so many different things.'

'The question is', said Humpty Dumpty, 'which is to be master – that's all.'   *Through the Looking-Glass*

They've a temper, some of them – particularly verbs:
they're the proudest – adjectives you can do anything
with, but not verbs – however, I can manage the whole
lot of them! Impenetrability! That's what I say!

Ibid.

I meant by 'impenetrability' that we've had enough of
that subject.

Ibid.

When I make a word do a lot of work like that ... I
always pay it extra.

Ibid.

They gave it me – for an un-birthday present.

Ibid.

When you've once said a thing, that fixes it, and you
must take the consequences.

Ibid.

'How is bread made?'
'I know *that*!' Alice cried eagerly. 'You take some
flour – '
'Where do you pick the flower?' the White Queen
asked: 'In a garden or in the hedges?'
'Well, it isn't *picked* at all,' Alice explained: 'it's
ground – '
'How many acres of ground?' said the White Queen.
'You mustn't leave out so many things.'

Ibid.

'I'm sure nobody walks much faster than I do!'
'He can't do that,' said the king, 'or else he'd have
been here first.'

Ibid.

Speak in French when you can't think of the English for
a thing.

Ibid.

'Twas brillig, and the slithy toves
Did gyre and gimble in the wabe:
All mimsy were the borogroves,
And the mome raths outgrabe.

Beware the Jabberwock, my son!
The jaws that bite, the claws that catch!
Beware the Jubjub bird, and shun
The frumious Bandersnatch!   *Ibid.*

'*Brillig*' means four o'clock in the afternoon – the time
when you begin *broiling* things for dinner.

Ibid.

'*Slithy*' means 'lithe and slimy'… You see it's like a
portmanteau – there are two meanings packed up into
one word.   *Ibid.*

'*Toves*' are something like badgers – they're something
like lizards – and they're something like corkscrews.

Ibid.

To '*gyre*' is to go round and round like a gyroscope. To
'*gimble*' is to make holes like a gimlet.

Ibid.

'*The wabe*' is the grass-plot round a sun-dial.

Ibid.

'*Mimsy*' is 'flimsy and miserable' (there's another
portmanteau for you). And a '*borogrove*' is a thin
shabby-looking bird with its feathers sticking out all
round – something like a live mop.

Ibid.

A '*rath*' is a sort of green pig: but '*mome*' I'm not certain
about. I think it's short for 'from home' – meaning that
they've lost their way, you know.

Ibid.

'*Outgribing*' is something between bellowing and whistling, with a kind of sneeze in the middle.

Ibid.

Why is it, I wonder, that I dote on the name Amelia more than any other word in the English language?

A Photographer's Day Out

'You shouldn't say "*us* put in a flower",' Sylvie very gravely remarked.

'Well, *hus*, then,' said Bruno. 'I never *can* remember those horrid H's!'

Sylvie and Bruno

'The Election shall be held without you.'
'Better so, than if it were held *within* me!'

Ibid.

'Give me your names.'
'We'd rather not!' Bruno exclaimed … 'We want them ourselves.'

Ibid.

What a comfort a Dictionary is!

Sylvie and Bruno Concluded

I wonder why they don't put some lumps of ice in the grate? … How jolly it would be to fill it now with lumps of ice, and sit round and enjoy the coolth!

Ibid.

It certainly is possible to say words so as to make them begin with capitals.

Ibid.

When I say 'yearned', I employ a word mildly expressive of what may be considered as an outline of my feelings in my calmer moments.

Novelty and Roman Cement

… autobiographical (a euphemism for 'egotistic').

Twelve Months in a Curatorship

Plain Anger is the inclination of two voters to one another, who meet together, but whose views are not in the same direction.   *The Dynamics of a Parti-cle*

Obtuse Anger is that which is greater than Right Anger.
          Ibid.

We are transfixed by the spectacle of Her Serene Brilliance, and bid an agonized farewell to her Condensed Milkiness.   *A Tangled Tale*

It is only a butler of experience who can manage three M's together, without any interjacent vowels.
          Ibid.

> Commencing every single phrase
> With 'therefore' or 'because',
> I blindly reeled, a hundred ways,
> About the syllogistic maze,
> Unconscious where I was.

          Phantasmagoria

> If you address a Ghost as 'Thing!'
> Or strike him with a hatchet,
> He is permitted by the King
> To drop all *formal* parleying –
> And you are *sure* to catch it!   *Ibid.*

Old Parallelepiped!   *Ibid.*

> And just as Sairey Gamp, for pains within,
> Administers a modicum of gin,
> So does my mind, when vexed and ill at ease,
> Console itself with soothing similes.

          Notes by an Oxford Chiel

Most things, you know, ought to be studied: even a trunk is studded with nails.

          Life and Letters

Children & Adults

Speak roughly to your little boy,
And beat him when he sneezes:
He only does it to annoy,
Because he knows it teases.

Alice in Wonderland

I speak severely to my boy,
And beat him when he sneezes:
For he can thoroughly enjoy
The pepper when he pleases!

Ibid.

'You are old, father William,' the young man said,
'And your hair has become very white;
And yet you incessantly stand on your head –
Do you think, at your age, it is right?'

'In my youth,' father William replied to his son,
'I feared it might injure the brain;
But, now that I'm perfectly sure I have none,
Why, I do it again and again.'

Ibid.

We are but older children.

Through the Looking-Glass

'Seven years and six months!' Humpty Dumpty repeated
thoughtfully. 'An uncomfortable sort of age. Now if
you'd asked my advice, I'd have said "Leave off at
seven" – but it's too late now.'

Ibid.

My Lady was a vast creature at all times: but, when she
frowned and folded her arms, as now, she looked more
gigantic than ever, and made one try to fancy what a
haystack would look like, if out of temper.

Sylvie and Bruno

A child's sorrow is violent, but short.

Ibid.

A hideous fat boy ... with the expression of a prize-pig.
Sylvie and Bruno Concluded

An old man's memory has but a slender hold on recent events.

Ibid.

What a pathetic beauty there is in the sweet fresh voices of the children, and how earnestly they sing!
The Lost Plum Cake

Real children – children who have not been spoiled by too much notice, and thus taught to give themselves the airs of little men and women.

Ibid.

> Ye golden hours of Life's young spring,
> Of innocence, of love and truth!
> Bright beyond all imagining,
> Thou fairy-dream of youth!
> *Three Sunsets and other Poems*

> I'd give all wealth that years have piled,
> The slow result of Life's decay,
> To be once more a little child
> For one bright summer-day.

Ibid.

> Peace dwells in those soft-lidded eyes,
> Those parted lips that faintly smile –
> Peace, the foretaste of Paradise,
> In heart too young for care or guile.

Ibid.

Man has his work, but what can woman do? ...
His is a path of thorns: he beats them down:
He faces death: he wrestles with despair.
Thine is of roses, to adorn and cheer
His lonely life, and hide the thorns in flowers.

Ibid.

The man that smiles – that reads *The Times* –
That goes to Christmas Pantomimes –
Is capable of *any* crimes!

Phantasmagoria

Ah, happy he who owns that tenderest joy,
The heart-love of a child!

Hunting of the Snark, preface

After the Russian children, whose type of face is ugly as
a rule, it is quite a relief to get back among the Germans
with their large eyes and delicate features.

Life and Letters

Next to what conversing with an angel might be – for it
is hard to imagine – comes, I think, the privilege of
having a real child's thoughts uttered to one.

Ibid.

I think that a child's first attitude to the world is a simple
love for all living things.

Ibid.

My best love to yourself, – to your Mother
My kindest regards – to your small
Fat, impertinent, ignorant brother
My hatred – I think that is all.

Ibid.

Poetry, Books & Writing

What is the use of a book … without pictures or conversations?

Alice in Wonderland

Perhaps the hardest thing in all literature – at least *I* have found it so: by no voluntary effort can I accomplish it: I have to take it as it comes – is to write anything *original*. And perhaps the easiest is, when once an original line has been struck out, to follow it up, and to write any amount more of the same.

Sylvie and Bruno, preface

If Shakespeare were not inspired, one may well doubt if any man ever was.

Ibid.

Neither Bowdler's, Chambers's, Brandram's, nor Cundell's 'Boudoir' Shakespeare, seems to me to meet the want: they are not sufficiently 'expurgated'. Bowdler's is the most extraordinary of all: looking through it, I am filled with a deep sense of wonder, considering what he has left in, that he should have cut *anything* out!

Ibid.

I am strongly of opinion that an author had far better not read any reviews of his books: the unfavourable ones are almost certain to make him cross, and the favourable ones conceited; and neither of these results is desirable.

Sylvie and Bruno Concluded

The slowest and most intermittent talker must *seem* fluent in letter-writing. He may have taken half-an-hour to *compose* his second sentence; but there it is, close after the first!

Ibid.

And would you be a poet
Before you've been to school?
Ah well! I hardly thought you
So absolute a fool.

Phantasmagoria

For first you write a sentence,
And then you chop it small;
Then mix the bits, and sort them out
Just as they chance to fall:
The order of the phrases makes
No difference at all.

Then if you'd be impressive,
Remember what I say,
That abstract qualities begin
With capitals alway:
The True, the Good, the Beautiful –
Those are the things that pay!

Next, when you are describing
A shape, or sound, or tint;
Don't state the matter plainly,
But put it in a hint;
And learn to look at all things
With a short of mental squint.

Ibid.

Such epithets, like pepper,
Give zest to what you write;
And, if you strew them sparely,
They whet the appetite:
But if you lay them on too thick,
You spoil the matter quite!   *Ibid.*

Where life becomes a Spasm,
And history a Whiz:
If that is not Sensation,
I won't know what it is.   *Ibid.*

My thirst and passion from boyhood ... has been for poetry – for poetry in its widest and wildest sense – for poetry untrammelled by the laws of sense, rhyme, or rhythm, soaring through the universe, and echoing the music of the spheres.

Novelty and Romancement

I said it in Hebrew – I said it in Dutch –
I said it in German and Greek:
But I wholly forgot (and it vexes me much)
That English is what you speak!

Hunting of the Snark

None but the best poetry will stand close printing and cheap paper.

Life and Letters

Words mean more than we mean to express when we use them; so a whole book ought to mean a great deal more than the writer means.

Ibid.

One of the hardest things in the world is to convey a meaning accurately from one mind to another.

Ibid.

Boasts, Exclamations & Exhortations

Oh my ears and whiskers! *Alice in Wonderland*

I'm older than you, and must know better. *Ibid.*

Oh my fur and whiskers! *Ibid.*

You're enough to try the patience of an oyster! *Ibid.*

Those serpents! There's no pleasing them! *Ibid.*

I never heard it before ... but it sounds uncommon nonsense. *Ibid.*

You're nothing but a pack of cards! *Ibid.*

Let's all move one place on. *Ibid.*

'I shall sit here,' he said, 'on and off, for days and days.' *Ibid.*

Just about as much right ... as pigs have to fly. *Ibid.*

Everything's got a moral if only you can find it. *Ibid.*

That's nothing to what I could say if I chose. *Ibid.*

You don't know much ... and that's a fact. *Ibid.*

I've seen gardens compared with which this would be a wilderness. *Through the Looking-Glass*

I could show you hills, in comparison with which you'd call that a valley.

Ibid.

I've heard nonsense, compared with which that would be as sensible as a dictionary.

Ibid.

One can't, perhaps ... but *two* can.   *Ibid.*

Imperial fiddlestick!   *Ibid.*

Sap and sawdust.   *Ibid.*

You won't make yourself a bit realer by crying.

Ibid.

I hope you don't suppose those are *real* tears?

Ibid.

There's glory for you!   *Ibid.*

I turned cold to the very ends of my whiskers.

Ibid.

O frabjous day!   *Ibid.*

Come to my arms, my beamish boy!   *Ibid.*

Nohow!   *Ibid.*

Contrariwise.   *Ibid.*

Consider anything, only don't cry!   *Ibid.*

Fit to snore his head off!   *Ibid.*

It's very provoking ... to be called an egg – *very*!

Ibid.

Now, *here*, you see, it takes all the running *you* can do, to keep in the same place. If you want to get somewhere else, you must run at least twice as fast as that.

Ibid.

Mind you come up – the regular way – don't get blown up!

Ibid.

If you do such a thing again, I'll have you buttered!

Ibid.

You might as well try to stop a Bandersnatch!

Ibid.

Sometimes I've believed as many as six impossible things before breakfast.

Ibid.

It's as large as life, and twice as natural.

Ibid.

It's a poor sort of memory that only works backwards.

Ibid.

To be able to see Nobody! And at that distance too! Why, it's as much as *I* can do to see real people.

Ibid.

I'm very brave generally ... only to-day I happen to have a headache.

Ibid.

I can explain all the poems that ever were invented – and a good many that haven't been invented just yet.

Ibid.

No admittance till the week after next!

Ibid.

He's a very learned doctor. Why, he's actually invented three new diseases, besides a new way of breaking your collar-bone!

Sylvie and Bruno

He's a wonderfully clever man, you know. Sometimes he says things that only the other Professor can understand. Sometimes he says things that *nobody* can understand!

Ibid.

All of me, that isn't Bonhomie, is Rumination.

Sylvie and Bruno Concluded

All of me, that is not Lumbago, is Loyalty!

Ibid.

Like two Grasshoppers in a volcano, we are shrivelled up in the presence of Her Spangled Vehemence!

A Tangled Tale

A knot ... Oh, do let me help to undo it!

Ibid.

You really must try to cultivate a more capacious mind.

Ibid.

What I tell you three times is true.

Hunting of the Snark

Christ Church stands convicted of two unpardonable crimes – being great, and having a name.

Life and Letters

Ironies

Curiouser and curiouser!

Alice in Wonderland

The more there is of mine, the less there is of yours.

Ibid.

How cheerfully he seems to grin,
And how neatly spreads his claws.
And welcomes little fishes in
With gently smiling jaws.

Ibid.

'I have answered three questions, and that is enough,'
Said his father; 'don't give yourself airs!
Do you think I can listen all day to such stuff?
Be off, or I'll kick you downstairs!'

Ibid.

'I can't explain *myself*, I'm afraid, sir,' said Alice,
'because I'm not myself, you see.'
'I don't see,' said the Caterpillar.

Ibid.

The rule is, jam to-morrow and jam yesterday – but
never jam to-day.

Through the Looking-Glass

It's jam every other day: to-day isn't any other day, you
know.

Ibid.

'I wish I could manage to be glad!' the Queen said. 'Only
I never can remember the rule.'

Ibid.

Tweedledum and Tweedledee
Agreed to have a battle;
For Tweedledum said Tweedledee
Had spoiled his nice new rattle.

Ibid.

Let's fight till six, and then have dinner.

Ibid.

'The horror of that moment,' the King went on, 'I shall never, *never* forget!'

'You will, though,' the Queen said, 'if you don't make a memorandum of it.'

Ibid.

Life, what is it but a dream?

Ibid.

Threescore years and ten, baldness and spectacles.

Sylvie and Bruno

> Man's little Day in haste we spend,
> And, from its merry noontide, send
> No glance to meet the silent end.

Ibid.

A thick stick in one's hand makes people respectful.

Ibid.

Is Life itself a dream, I wonder?

Ibid.

They were not of the folk we meet in fashionable drawing rooms – who conceal all such feelings as they may chance to possess beneath the impenetrable mask of a conventional placidity. 'The Man with the Iron Mask' was, no doubt, a rarity and a marvel in his own age: in modern London no one would turn his head to give him a second look.

Ibid.

To most of us Life and its pleasures seem like a mine that is nearly worked out.

Ibid.

We lapse very quickly into nonsense.   *Ibid.*

> You're safe from being overfed:
> You're sweetly picturesque in rags:
> You never know the aching head
> That comes with money-bags:
> And you have time to cultivate
> That best of qualities, Content –
> For which you'll find your present state
> Remarkably convenient!   *Ibid.*

When a man's tipsy ... he sees one thing as two. But
when he's extremely sober ... he sees two things as one.
It's equally inconvenient, whichever happens.   *Ibid.*

> What you call healthy appetite
> I feel as Hunger's savage tooth:
> And, when no dinner is in sight,
> The dinner-bell's a sound of ruth.   *Ibid.*

> 'One can't be too deliberate',
> Said Paul, 'in parting with one's pelf.
> With bills, as you correctly state,
> I'm punctuality itself.
> A man may surely claim his dues:
> But, when there's money to be lent,
> A man must be allowed to choose
> Such times as are convenient!'   *Ibid.*

Life is indeed a drama: a drama with but few *encores* –
and no *bouquets* ... We spend half of it regretting the
things we did in the other half!   *Ibid.*

... office-hours – which I suppose reduce most men to
the mental condition of a coffee-mill or a mangle.

Sylvie and Bruno Concluded

It's a miserable story ... It begins miserably, and it ends
miserablier.   *Ibid.*

In giving birthday-presents, *my* motto is – cheapness!

Ibid.

The *great* thing to aim at was, that the Candidate should know absolutely *nothing* about the needs of the Examination.

Ibid.

What would medicine be, if it wasn't nasty?

Ibid.

Human life seems, on the whole, to contain more of sorrow than of joy. And yet the world goes on. Who knows why?

Ibid.

The character of a 'lunatic' is not, I believe, very difficult to *acquire*: but it is amazingly difficult to *get rid of*.

Ibid.

The period of life between the ages of a hundred-and-sixty-five and a hundred-and-seventy-five is a specially *safe* one … Am I not right in thinking that you never heard of any one dying between those two ages?

Ibid.

Those, who have never felt the anxiety, cannot fully realize the relief.

Three Years in a Curatorship

Long and painful experience has taught me one great principle in managing business for other people, *viz.*, if you want to inspire confidence, *give plenty of statistics*. It does not matter that they should be accurate, or even intelligible, so long as there is enough of them.

Ibid.

When an examiner is himself dimly hovering between a second class and a third, how is he to decide the position of others?

A Tangled Tale

Oh, do not forget the day when we met
At the fruiterer's shop in the city:
When you *said* I was plain and excessively vain,
But I knew that you *meant* I was pretty.

College Rhymes

He had forty-two boxes, all carefully packed,
With his name printed clearly on each:
But, since he omitted to mention the fact,
They were all left behind on the beach.

Hunting of the Snark

O bitter is it to abide
In weariness alway:
At dawn to sigh for eventide,
At eventide for day.
Thy noon hath fled: thy sun hath shone:
The brightness of the day is gone:
What need to lag and linger on
Till life be cold and gray?

Three Sunsets and other Poems

And cannot pleasures, while they last,
Be actual unless, when past,
They leave us shuddering and aghast,
With anguish smarting?
And cannot friends be firm and fast,
And yet bear parting.

Phantasmagoria

Don't be in such a hurry to believe next time – I'll tell
you why. If you set to work to believe everything, you
will tire out the muscles of your mind, and then you'll be
so weak you won't be able to believe the simplest true
things.

Life and Letters

Because you have invited me, therefore I cannot come.

Ibid.

Logic & Philosophy

Do cats eat bats? ... Do bats eat cats? ... As she couldn't answer either question, it didn't much matter which way she put it.

Alice in Wonderland

If you cut your finger *very* deeply with a knife, it usually bleeds.

Ibid.

If you drink much from a bottle marked 'poison', it is almost certain to disagree with you, sooner or later.

Ibid.

She tried to fancy what the flame of a candle looks like after the candle is blown out, for she could not remember ever having seen such a thing.

Ibid.

Was I the same when I got up this morning? I almost think I can remember feeling a little different. But if I'm not the same, the next question is 'Who in the world am I?' Ah, that's the great puzzle!

Ibid.

The best way to explain it is to do it.

Ibid.

If I don't take this child away with me ... they're sure to kill it in a day or two. Wouldn't it be murder to leave it behind?

Ibid.

'Would you tell me, please, which way I ought to go from here?'

'That depends a good deal on where you want to get to,' said the Cat.

'I don't much care where – ' said Alice.

'Then it doesn't matter which way you go,' said the Cat.

' – so long as I get *somewhere*,' Alice added as an explanation.

'Oh, you're sure to do that,' said the Cat, 'if you only walk long enough.'

Ibid.

'You should say what you mean,' the March Hare went on.

'I do,' Alice hastily replied; 'at least – at least I mean what I say – that's the same thing, you know.'

'Not the same thing a bit!' said the Hatter. 'Why, you might just as well say that "I see what I eat" is the same as "I eat what I see"!'

'You might just as well say,' added the March Hare, 'that "I like what I get" is the same thing as "I get what I like"!'

'You might just as well say,' added the Dormouse, which seemed to be talking in its sleep, that "I breathe when I sleep" is the same thing as "I sleep when I breathe"!'

Ibid.

'Take some more tea,' the March Hare said to Alice, very earnestly.

'I've had nothing yet,' Alice replied in an offended tone: 'so I can't take more.'

'You mean you can't take *less*,' said the Hatter: 'it's very easy to take more than nothing.'

Ibid.

'Begin at the beginning', the King said, very gravely, 'and go on till you come to the end: then stop.'

Ibid.

'That's not a regular rule: you invented it just now.'
'It's the oldest rule in the book,' said the King.
'Then it ought to be Number One,' said Alice.

Ibid.

Never imagine yourself not to be otherwise than what it might appear to others that what you were or might have been was not otherwise than what you had been would have appeared to them to be otherwise.

Ibid.

If it was so, it might be; and if it were so, it would be; but as it isn't it ain't. That's logic.

Through the Looking-Glass

'Why do you sit out here all alone?' said Alice, not wishing to begin an argument.

'Why, because there's nobody with me!' cried Humpty Dumpty. 'Did you think I didn't know the answer to *that*? Ask another.'

Ibid.

The sea was wet as wet could be,
The sands were dry as dry.
You could not see a cloud, because
No cloud was in the sky:
No birds were flying overhead –
There were no birds to fly.

Ibid.

You can look in front of you, and on both sides, if you like ... but you can't look *all* round you – unless you've got eyes at the back of your head.

Ibid.

It's one of the most serious things that can possibly happen to one in a battle – to get one's head cut off.

Ibid.

If you can see whether I'm singing or not, you've sharper eyes than most.

Ibid.

'There's nothing like eating hay when you're faint,' he remarked to her, as he munched away.

'I should think throwing cold water over you would be better,' Alice suggested: '– or some sal-volatile.'

'I didn't say there was nothing *better*,' the King replied. 'I said there was nothing *like* it.'

Ibid.

'Speak when you're spoken to!' the Queen sharply interrupted her.

'But if everybody obeyed that rule,' said Alice, who was always ready for a little argument, 'and if you only spoke when you're spoken to, and the other person always waited for *you* to begin, you see nobody would ever say anything.'

Ibid.

'Take a bone from a dog: what remains?'

Alice considered. 'The bone wouldn't remain: of course, if I took it – and the dog wouldn't remain: it would come to bite me – and I'm sure I shouldn't remain.'

'Then you think nothing would remain?' said the Red Queen.

'I think that's the answer.'

'Wrong, as usual,' said the Red Queen: 'the dog's temper would remain.'

'But I don't see how – '

'Why, look here!' the Red Queen cried. 'The dog would lose its temper, wouldn't it? ... Then if the dog went away, its temper would remain!'

Ibid.

'I'm sure I didn't mean – ' Alice was beginning, but the Red Queen interrupted her impatiently.

'That's just what I complain of! You *should* have meant! What do you suppose is the use of a child without any meaning? Even a joke should have some meaning – and a child's more important than a joke, I hope. You couldn't deny that, even if you tried with both hands.'

'I don't deny things with my *hands*,' Alice objected.

'Nobody said you did,' said the Red Queen. 'I said you couldn't if you tried.'

Ibid.

'The name of the song is called "Haddocks' Eyes".'

'Oh, that's the name of the song, is it?' Alice said, trying to feel interested.

'No, you don't understand,' the Knight said, looking a little vexed. 'That's what the name is *called*. The name really is "*The Aged Aged Man*".'

'Then I ought to have said "That's what the *song* is called"?' Alice corrected herself.

'No, you oughtn't: that's quite another thing! The *song* is called "Ways and Means": but that's only what it's *called*, you know!'

'Well, what *is* the song, then?' said Alice, who was by this time completely bewildered.

'I was coming to that,' the Knight said. 'The song really is "*A-sitting On A Gate*": and the tune's my own invention.'

Ibid.

Things that are greater than the same are greater than one another.

Sylvie and Bruno

It's impossible to read *here*, for all my books are in the house.

Ibid.

Nothing can be *heavy*, you know, except by *trying* to fall, and being prevented from doing so.

Ibid.

The *First* Axiom ... consists of these words, '*Whatever is, is.*' And the Second consists of *these* words, '*Whatever isn't, isn't.*'

Sylvie and Bruno Concluded

In Science – in fact, in most things – it is usually best *to begin at the beginning*. In *some* things, of course, it's better to begin at the *other* end. For instance, if you wanted to paint a dog green, it *might* be best to begin with the *tail*, as it doesn't bite at *that* end.

Ibid.

When in doubt ... take an extreme case.

A Tangled Tale

Problem. – The Governor of Kgovjni wants to give a very small dinner party, and invites his father's brother-in-law, his brother's father-in-law, his father-in-law's brother, and his brother-in-law's father. Find the number of guests.
Answer. – One.

Ibid.

If you make an infinite noise, you'll get no jam: and if you make no noise, you'll get an infinite lot of jam.

Ibid.

When I come upon anything – in Logic or in any other hard subject – that entirely puzzles me, I find it a capital plan to talk it over, *aloud*, even when I am all alone. One can explain things so *clearly* to one's self! And then, you know, one is so *patient* with one's self: one *never* gets irritated at one's own stupidity.

Symbolic Logic

No bald person needs a hair-brush;
No lizards have hair;
Therefore no lizard needs a hair-brush.

The Game of Logic

Caterpillars are not eloquent;
Jones is eloquent;
Therefore Jones is not a caterpillar.

Ibid.

Query: when we are dreaming and, as often happens, have a dim consciousness of the fact and try to wake, do we not say and do things which in waking life would be insane? May we not then sometimes define insanity as an inability to distinguish which is the waking and which the sleeping life? We often dream without the least suspicion of unreality: 'Sleep hath its own world', and it is often as lifelike as the other.

Life and Letters

The consumption of Madeira has been during the past year, zero. After careful calculation I estimate that, if this rate of consumption be steadily maintained, our present stock will last us an infinite number of years.

Ibid.

I'm so glad I don't like asparagus ... because if I *did* like it, I should have to eat it – and I can't bear it!

Ibid.

Eating & Drinking

Do let's pretend that I'm a hungry hyaena, and you're a bone!

Alice in Wonderland

Beautiful soup! Who cares for fish,
Game, or any other dish?
Who would not give all else for two p
ennyworth only of Beautiful Soup?
Pennyworth only of Beautiful Soup?

Beau-ootiful Soo-oop!
Beau-ootiful Soo-oop!
Soo-oop of the e-e-evening,
Beautiful, beauti-FUL SOUP!

Ibid.

Then fill up the glasses as quick as you can,
And sprinkle the table with buttons and bran:
Put cats in the coffee and mice in the tea –
And welcome Queen Alice with thirty-times-three!

Through the Looking-Glass

Then fill up the glasses with treacle and ink,
Or anything else that is pleasant to drink:
Mix sand with the cider, and wool with the wine –
And welcome Queen Alice with ninety-times-nine!

Ibid.

Cherry-jam is best, for mere *chiaroscuro* of flavour: *raspberry*-jam lends itself best to those resolved discords that linger so lovingly on the tongue: but, for rapturous *utterness* of saccharine perfection, it's *apricot-jam first and the rest nowhere*!

Sylvie and Bruno Concluded

If you want to *see* a man, offer him something to eat. It's the same with a mouse.

Ibid.

Take my friends and my home – as an outcast I'll
   roam,
Take the money I have in the Bank;
It is just what I wish, but deprive me of *fish*,
And my life would indeed be a blank!

Early Verse

How blest would be
A life so free –
Ipwergis-Pudding to consume
And drink the subtle Azzigoom.

Ibid.

He goes about and sits on folk
That eat too much at night:
His duties are to pinch, and poke,
And squeeze them till they nearly choke.
(I said 'It serves them right!')

Phantasmagoria

If you like your coffee with sand for dregs,
A decided hint of salt in your tea,
And a fishy taste in the very eggs –
By all means choose the sea.

Ibid.

Dancing & General Jubilation

Everybody has won, and *all* must have prizes!

Alice in Wonderland

The Lobster Quadrille.

Ibid.

Advance twice, set to partners ... change lobsters, and
retire in same order.

Ibid.

Will you, won't you, will you, won't you, will you join
 the dance?
Will you, won't you, will you, won't you, won't you
 join the dance?

Ibid.

The further off from England the nearer is to France –
Then turn not pale, beloved snail, but come and join
 the dance.

Ibid.

He chortled in his joy.

Through the Looking-Glass

'To be or not to be!' Hamlet remarked in a cheerful tone,
and then turned head-over-heels several times.

Sylvie and Bruno

The music of Midsummer madness
Shall sting him with many a bite,
Till, in rapture of rollicking sadness,
He shall groan with a gloomy delight:
He shall swathe him, like mists of the morning,
In platitudes luscious and limp,
Such as decks, with a deathless adorning,
The Song of the Shrimp!

Sylvie and Bruno Concluded

Religion & Morality

She generally gave herself very good advice (though she very seldom followed it), and sometimes she scolded herself so severely as to bring tears into her eyes; and once she remembered trying to box her own ears for having cheated herself in a game of croquet she was playing against herself.   *Alice in Wonderland*

Hard work and endurance of privations are no proof of an unselfish motive.
                              Popular Fallacies about Vivisection

We may safely take our stand on the principle of doing the duty which we see before us; secondary consequences are at once out of our control and beyond our calculation.   *Ibid.*

The man whose sympathies have been deadened, and whose selfishness has been fostered, by the contemplation of pain deliberately inflicted, may be the parent of others equally brutalized, and so bequeath a curse to future ages.   *Ibid.*

Even if we limit our view to the present time, who can doubt that the degradation of a soul is a greater evil than the suffering of bodily frame?   *Ibid.*

It is a humiliating but an undeniable truth, that man has something of the wild beast in him, that a thirst for blood can be aroused in him by witnessing a scene of carnage, and that the infliction of torture, when the first instincts of horror have been deadened by the familiarity, may become, first, a matter of indifference, then a subject of morbid interest, then a positive pleasure, and then a ghastly and ferocious delight.   *Ibid.*

If the thought of sudden death acquires, *for you*, a special horror when imagined as happening in a *theatre*, then be very sure the theatre is harmful for *you*, however harmless it may be for others; and that *you* are incurring a deadly peril in going. Be sure the safest rule is that we should not dare to *live* in any scene in which we dare not *die*.

Sylvie and Bruno

> He either fears his fate too much
> Or his desert is small,
> Who does not put it to the touch,
> To win or lose it all.

Ibid.

For generous appreciation of all one's *best* qualities ... there's nothing to compare with a father.

Ibid.

You can't mean to say that Fairies are never greedy, or selfish, or cross, or deceitful, because that would be nonsense, you know. Well then, don't you think they might be all the better for a little lecturing and punishment now and then?

Ibid.

We should learn to take our pleasures *quickly* and our pains *slowly*.

Ibid.

Can you have a stronger proof of the Original Goodness there must be in this nation, than the fact that Religion has been preached to us as a commercial speculation, for a century, and that we still believe in a God?

Ibid.

A man who gratifies every fancy that occurs to him – denying himself in *nothing* – and merely gives to the poor some part, or even *all*, of his *superfluous* wealth, is only deceiving himself if he calls it charity.

Sylvie and Bruno Concluded

God has given to Man an absolute right to take the *lives* of other animals, for any reasonable cause, such as the supply of food: but ... He has *not* given to Man the right to inflict *pain*, unless when necessary: ... mere pleasure, or advantage, does not constitute such a necessity: ... and, consequently, ... pain inflicted for the purposes of *sport*, is cruel and therefore wrong.   *Ibid.*

How slight the barriers seem to be that part Christian from Christian, when one has to deal with the great facts of Life and the reality of Death!   *Ibid.*

(N.B. If I have a virtue, it is quiet, gentlemanly caution.)
                    A Photographer's Day Out

There are sceptical thoughts, which seem for the moment to uproot the firmest faith: there are blasphemous thoughts, which dart unbidden into the most reverent souls; there are unholy thoughts, which torture, with their hateful presence, the fancy that would fain be pure. Against all these some real mental work is a most helpful ally.   *Pillow Problems*

Do thou thy task, and leave the rest to God.
                    Three Sunsets and Other Poems

> Who let the thought of bliss denied
> Make havoc of our life and powers,
> And pine, in solitary pride,
> For peace that never shall be ours,
> Because we will not work and wait
> In trustful patience for our fate.
>
>   *Ibid.*

We are not intended to rest content in any pleasure of earth, however intense: the yearning has been wisely given us, which points to an eternity of happiness, as the only perfect happiness possible.
                    Life and Letters

If you limit your actions in life to things that *nobody* can possibly find fault with, you will not do much.

Ibid.

A working life is a happy one.

Ibid.

Of all virtues a waiter can display, that of a retiring disposition is quite the least desirable.

Ibid.

Can a man who has once realised by minute study what the nerves are, what the brain is, and what waves of agony the one can convey to the other, go forth and wantonly inflict pain on any sentient being?

Ibid.

Selfishness is the keynote of all purely secular education.

Ibid.

There is sadness in coming to the end of anything in life. Man's instincts cling to the Life that will never end.

Ibid.

More and more it seems to me ... that what a person *is* is of more importance in God's sight than merely what propositions he affirms or denies.

Ibid.

While the laughter of *joy* is in full harmony with our deeper life, the laughter of amusement should be kept apart from it.

Ibid.

On Himself

And what means all these mysteries to me
Whose life is so full of indices and surds?

$$X^2 + 7X + 53 = 1\tfrac{1}{3}$$

Phantasmagoria

I am fond of children (except boys).

Life and Letters

Boys ... are a mistake.

Ibid.

As to dancing, my dear, I *never* dance, unless I am
allowed to do it *in my own peculiar way*. There is no use
trying to describe it: it has to be seen to be believed. The
last house I tried it in, the floor broke through. But then
it was a poor sort of floor – the beams were only six
inches thick, hardly worth calling beams at all: stone
arches are much more sensible, when any dancing, *of my
peculiar kind*, is to be done. Did you ever see the
Rhinoceros, and the Hippopotamus, at the Zoological
Gardens, trying to dance a minuet together? It is a
touching sight.

Ibid.

I'm not an at-homely man.

Ibid.

Sometimes I go to bed again a minute before I get up!
Did you ever hear of any one being so tired as that?

Ibid.

I cannot say that I look back on my life at a Public School
with any sensations of pleasure, or that any earthly
consideration would induce me to go through my three
years again.

Ibid.

Great mercies, great failings, time lost, talents
misapplied – such has been the past year.

Ibid.

A year of great blessings and few trials, of much
weakness and sin: yet I trust I have learned to know
myself better, and have striven (yet how feebly and
ineffectually) to live nearer to God.

Ibid.

I can imagine no more delightful occupation than
brushing Ellen Terry's hair!

Ibid.

Usually the child becomes so entirely a different being as
she grows into a woman, that our friendship has to
change too: and that it usually does by gliding down
from a loving intimacy into an acquaintance that merely
consists of a smile and a bow when we meet!

Ibid.

Animals & Plants

She considered him to be a footman because he was in livery: otherwise, judging by his face only, she would have called him a fish.   *Alice in Wonderland*

If it had grown up ... it would have made a dreadfully ugly child: but it makes rather a handsome pig, I think.
Ibid.

It is a very inconvenient habit of kittens ... that, whatever you say to them, they *always* purr ... How can you talk with a person if they *always* say the same thing?
Ibid.

Twinkle, twinkle, little bat!
How I wonder what you're at!

Ibid.

We call him Tortoise because he taught us.

Ibid.

'I've often seen a cat without a grin,' thought Alice; 'but a grin without a cat! It's the most curious thing I ever saw in all my life!'   *Ibid.*

Alice thought she had never seen such a curious croquet ground in her life: it was all ridges and furrows: the croquet balls were live hedgehogs, and the mallets live flamingoes, and the soldiers had to double themselves up and stand on their hands and feet, to make the arches.
Ibid.

'In most gardens', the Tiger-lily said, 'they make the beds too soft – so that the flowers are always asleep.'
Ibid.

'Will you walk a little faster?' said the whiting to a
    snail,
'There's a porpoise close behind us, and he's treading
    on my tail.'

Ibid.

'Tis the voice of the lobster; I heard him declare,
'You have baked me too brown, I must sugar my hair.'

Ibid.

'Have you seen the Mock Turtle yet?'
   'No,' said Alice. 'I don't even know what a Mock
Turtle is.'
   'It's the thing Mock Turtle soup is made from,' said
the Queen.

Ibid.

The Walrus and the Carpenter
Were walking close at hand:
They wept like anything to see
Such quantities of sand:
'If this were only cleared away,'
They said, 'it *would* be grand.'

'If seven maids with seven mops
Swept it for half a year,
Do you suppose', the Walrus said,
'That they would get it clear?'
'I doubt it,' said the Carpenter,
And shed a bitter tear.

Through the Looking-Glass

Four young oysters hurried up,
All eager for the treat:
Their coats were brushed, their faces washed,
Their shoes were clean and neat –
And this was odd, because, you know,
They hadn't any feet.

Ibid.

'The time has come,' the Walrus said,
'To talk of many things:
Of shoes – and ships – and sealing-wax –
Of cabbages – and kings –
Of why the sea is boiling hot –
And whether pigs have wings.'   *Ibid.*

He said 'I look for butterflies
That sleep among the wheat:
I make them into mutton-pies,
And sell them in the street.
I sell them unto men,' he said,
'Who sail on stormy seas;
And that's the way I make my bread –
A trifle, if you please.'   *Ibid.*

He said 'I hunt for haddocks' eyes
Among the heather bright,
And work them into waistcoat-buttons
In the silent night.
And these I do not sell for gold
Or coin of silvery shine,
But for a copper halfpenny,
And that will purchase nine.   *Ibid.*

He thought he saw an Elephant,
That practised on a fife:
He looked again, and found it was
A letter from his wife.
'At last I realise,' he said,
'The bitterness of Life!'

          Sylvie and Bruno

He thought he saw a Buffalo
Upon the chimney-piece:
He looked again, and found it was
His Sister's Husband's niece.
'Unless you leave the house,' he said,
'I'll send for the Police!'   *Ibid.*

He thought he saw a Rattlesnake
That questioned him in Greek:
He looked again, and found it was
The Middle of Next Week.
'The one thing I regret,' he said,
'Is that it cannot speak!'

Ibid.

He thought he saw a Kangaroo
That worked a coffee-mill:
He looked again, and found it was
A Vegetable-Pill,
'Were I to swallow this,' he said,
'I should be very ill!'

Ibid.

He thought he saw a Banker's Clerk
Descending from the bus:
He looked again, and found it was
A Hippopotamus:
'If this should stay to dine,' he said,
'There won't be much for us!'

Ibid.

He thought he saw an Albatross
That followed round the lamp:
He looked again, and found it was
A penny-postage stamp.
'You'd best be getting home,' he said,
'The nights are very damp!'

Ibid.

He thought he saw a Coach-and-Four
That stood beside his bed:
He looked again, and found it was
A Bear without a Head.
'Poor thing,' he said, 'poor silly thing!
It's waiting to be fed!'

Ibid.

A swarm of bees is simply a single animal whose many limbs are not quite close together.

Sylvie and Bruno Concluded

Dead mouses *never* objecks to be eaten.

Ibid.

Little Birds are playing
Bagpipes on the shore,
Where the tourists snore:
'Thanks!' they cry. ''Tis thrilling
Take, oh, take this shilling!
Let us have no more!'

Early Verse

We lived beneath the mat.
Warm and snug and fat,
But one woe, and that
Was the cat!

Life and Letters

Love & Pleasure

'Oh, 'tis love, 'tis love, that makes the world go round!'
'Somebody said,' Alice whispered, 'that it's done by everybody minding their own business.'
'Ah, well! It means much the same thing,' said the Duchess.

Alice in Wonderland

I wonder if the snow loves the trees and fields, that it kisses them so gently?

Through the Looking-Glass

We lose half the pleasure we might have in life, by not really attending.

Sylvie and Bruno

The only really *unsuitable* matches ... are those made without sufficient *Money*. Love may come afterwards. Money is needed *to begin with*!

Sylvie and Bruno Concluded

As no topic seemed to occur to any one, and as we were, all four, on those delightful terms with one another (the only terms, I think, on which any friendship, that deserves the name of *intimacy*, can be maintained) which involves no sort of necessity for *speaking* for mere speaking's sake, we sat in silence.

Ibid.

... that wayward smooth-flowing current of chat about nothing in particular, which is perhaps the most enjoyable of all forms of conversation.

The Blank Cheque

There was a young lady of station,
'I love man' was her sole exclamation;
But when men cried, 'You flatter,'
She replied, 'Oh! no matter,
Isle of Man is the true explanation.'

Acrostics and other Verses

The best work a man can do is when he works for love's
sake only, with no thought of fame or gain or earthly
reward.   *Life and Letters*

I almost held my breath to watch: the illusion is perfect,
and I felt as if in a dream all the time that it lasted. It was
like a delicious reverie, or the most beautiful poetry. This
is the true end and object of acting – to raise the mind
above itself, and out of its petty cares.   *Ibid.*

It was a lovely Autumn evening, and the glorious effects
of dramatic aberration were beginning to show
themselves in the atmosphere as the earth revolved
away from the great western luminary, when two lines
might have been observed wending their weary way
across a plane superficies. The elder of the two had by
long practice acquired the art, so painful to young and
impulsive loci, of lying evenly between his extreme
points; but the younger, in her girlish impetuosity, was
ever longing to diverge and become a hyperbola or some
such romantic and boundless curve. They had lived and
loved: fate and the intervening superficies had hitherto
kept them asunder, but this was no longer to be: a line
had intersected them making the two interior angles
together less than two right angles. It was a moment
never to be forgotten.   *The Dynamics of a Parti-cle*

Love stretches hands from shore to shore:
Love is, and shall not perish!   *Life and Letters*

… loving as a dog (forgive the prosaic simile, but I know
no earthly love so pure and perfect).   *Ibid.*

Nonsense & Riddles

Flamingoes and mustard both bite. And the moral is –
'Birds of a feather flock together.'

Alice in Wonderland

Why is a raven like a writing-desk?

Ibid.

'I think you might do something better with the time,'
she said, 'than wasting it in asking riddles that have no
answer.'
'If you knew Time as well as I do,' said the Hatter,
'you wouldn't talk about wasting *it*. It's *him*.'

Ibid.

Maybe it's always pepper that makes people
hot-tempered ... and vinegar that makes them sour –
and camomile that makes them bitter – and – and
barley-sugar and such things that make children
sweet-tempered.

Ibid.

If you'll believe in me, I'll believe in you. Is that a
bargain?

Through the Looking-Glass

I don't like belonging to another person's dream ... I've a
great mind to go and wake him, and see what happens!

Ibid.

If he smiles much more the ends of his mouth might
meet behind ... And then I don't know *what* would
happen to his head! I'm afraid it would come off!

Ibid.

He's an Anglo-Saxon Messenger – and those are Anglo-Saxon attitudes. He only does them when he's happy.   *Ibid.*

The other Messenger's called Hatta. I must have *two*, you know – to come and to go. One to come, and one to go.
                                                         Ibid.

The more head downwards I am, the more I keep inventing new things.
                                                         Ibid.

One, two! One, two! and through and through
The vorpal blade went snicker-snack!
He left it dead, and with its head
He went galumphing back.
                                                         Ibid.

The sun was shining on the sea,
Shining with all his might:
He did his very best to make
The billows smooth and bright –
And this was odd, because it was
The middle of the night.

The moon was shining sulkily,
Because she thought the sun
Had got no business to be there
After the day was done –
'It's very rude of him,' she said,
'To come and spoil the fun!'   *Ibid.*

Which is easiest to do,
Un-dish-cover the fish, or dishcover the riddle?
                                                         Ibid.

Why shouldn't I walk on my own forehead?
                                              Sylvie and Bruno

There's the rabbit-hutch and the hall-clock ... One gets a little confused with *them* – both having doors, you know. Now, only yesterday – would you believe it? – I put some lettuces into the clock, and tried to wind up the rabbit!

Ibid.

All extremes are bad ... For instance, Sobriety is a very good thing, when practised in *moderation*: but even Sobriety, when carried to an *extreme*, has its disadvantages.

Ibid.

I don't believe in Fairies with wings.

Ibid.

A Man's severe thinking, plus the shaking-off a cigar-ash, comes to the same total as a Woman's trivial fancies, *plus* the most elaborate embroidery.

Ibid.

The *Medicine*'s the great thing, you know. You can keep a *Medicine*, for years and years: but nobody ever wants to keep a *Disease*.'

Ibid.

We have gone on selecting *walking-sticks* – always keeping those that walked *best* – till we have obtained some that can walk by themselves!

Ibid.

> He thought he saw an Argument
> That proved he was the Pope:
> He looked again, and found it was
> A Bar of Mottled Soap.
> 'A fact so dread' he faintly said,
> 'Extinguishes all hope!'

Ibid.

There was a young man of Oporta,
Who daily got shorter and shorter.
The reason he said
Was the hod on his head
Which was filled with the *heaviest* mortar.

Early Verse

I dreamt I dwelt in marble halls,
And each damp thing that crawls and crawls
Went wobble-wobble on the walls.   *Ibid.*

He was thoughtful and grave – but the orders he gave
Were enough to bewilder a crew.
When he cried 'Steer to starboard but keep her head
    larboard!'
What on earth was the helmsman to do?

Hunting of the Snark

He would answer to 'Hi!' or to any loud cry,
Such as 'Fry me!' or 'Fritter my wig!'
To 'What-you-may-call-um!' or 'What-was-his-name!'
But especially 'Thing-um-a-jig!'   *Ibid.*

In the midst of the word he was trying to say,
In the midst of his laughter and glee,
He had softly and suddenly vanished away –
For the Snark *was* a Boojum, you see.   *Ibid.*

Who can tell whether the parallelogram, which in our
ignorance we have defined and drawn, and the whole of
whose properties we profess to know, may not be all the
while panting for exterior angles, sympathetic with the
interior, or sullenly repining at the fact that it cannot be
inscribed in a circle?   *The Dynamics of a Parti-cle*

A Russian had three sons. The first, named Rab, became
a lawyer; the second, Ymra, became a soldier; the third
became a sailor. What has his name?

Life and Letters